this journal belongs to:

May taking care
of yourself
show you how
valuable you truly are.
You are deserving
of the love
you pour out into
the world.

What do I need today?

_____

_____

How do I feel today?

_____

_____

Who am I today?

_____

_____

In what ways do I need support today?

_____

_____

What am I releasing today?

_____

_____

What am I standing in today?

_____

_____

How am I celebrating myself today?

_____

_____

How am I blooming today?

_____

_____

In what ways can I celebrate myself more?

_____

_____

How am I unfolding as I move through my healing?

_____

_____

In what ways can I listen to my intuition more?

_____

_____

How can I make myself feel safe enough to unfold and let go?

_____

_____

How can I stand in my truth in a way that honors my past and acknowledges my future?

_____

_____

What do I need to feel free in this moment?

_____

_____

What do I need to unpack to prepare for joy?

_____

_____

How is happiness showing up in my life these days?

_____

_____

Who is holding me back?

_____

_____

How can I reshape my narrative?

_____

_____

What am I scared of when it comes to pursuing my desires?

_____

_____

When do I lean into my truth the most?

_____

_____

What is sacred to me lately?

_____

_____

How am I cherishing my time and where I invest it?

_____

_____

Aside from myself, who can I lean on to hold me accountable in my evolution?

_____

_____

How can I use my gifts to serve others?

_____

_____

Draw a circle below, write the things you need inside of it.
Anything you don't need, or wish to keep out,
write it on the outside of the circle.

Make a list of what you need to be supported in this moment.

1. _____

2. _____

3. _____

4. _____

5. _____

Write a self-love letter below to your younger self
centered around self-trust and perseverance.

Dear Self,

Make a list of what you need to feel heard.

1. _____

2. _____

3. _____

4. _____

5. _____

Draw a picture of a flower garden.
On each of your flowers' petals, write what you wish to see
come to fruition.

Fill this page with Affirmations

I am _____

I will _____

I can _____

I am _____

I will _____

I can _____

I am _____

I will _____

I can _____

I am _____

I will _____

I can _____

Fill this page with dreams and ambitions.
Use color and get creative!

How am I feeding my soul so that joy can show up and flourish?

_____

_____

_____

_____

_____

_____

_____

_____

_____

_____

_____

_____

Write a self-love letter centered around belonging and understanding.

Dear Self,

Calligraphy Style
Use this guide to help you create beautiful lettering.

A B C D E F

G H I J K L

M N O P Q R

L T U V W

X Y Z

a b c d e f g h i j k l m n
o p q r s t u v w x y z

0 1 2 3 4 5 6 7 8 9

write out your one word affirmation:

manifestation of the week:

manifestation of the week:

manifestation of the week:

manifestation of the week:

33636463R00031

Made in the USA
Columbia, SC
20 November 2018